LIMERICKS, LESSONS, AND LIFE IN HANDBELLS

BY KEVIN McCHESNEY

INFINITY
PUBLISHING

Copyright © 2011 by Kevin McChesney
Registration Number: TX 7-423-114

ISBN 978-0-7414-6686-0 Paperback
ISBN 978-0-7414-6687-7 Hardcover
ISBN 978-0-7414-9488-7 eBook

Printed in the United States of America

Published January 2013

INFINITY PUBLISHING
1094 New DeHaven Street, Suite 100
West Conshohocken, PA 19428-2713
Toll-free (877) BUY BOOK
Local Phone (610) 941-9999
Fax (610) 941-9959
Info@buybooksontheweb.com
www.buybooksontheweb.com

DEDICATION

I owe a great debt of thanks to the thousands of ringers and directors who have shared their gifts, enthusiasm, and spirit with me throughout my years in handbells. They've allowed me to compose, teach, and direct with embracing generosity, and it is their eagerness to grow in artistry and ministry that has inspired whatever insights and creativity I might humbly offer. This book is dedicated, with gratitude, to these true heroes of our art.

And, of course,…

I have a companion and wife
Who sees me through joy and through strife.
She brightens my days,
And in thousands of ways
Writes the music that makes up my life.

Thank you, Tracy…well, for everything.

ACKNOWLEDGEMENT

Many fond thanks to Megan Reishus for her tremendous editorial skills and for contributing numerous ideas to make this project complete. Friends like her make both work and life more fun.

INTRODUCTION

One of the interesting "musical" challenges of reading through these limericks (as well as of composing them) is to work out where the accents go. Limericks are in a natural, sing-song form – that's what makes them limericks. To make some teaching points work, as well as to get certain sentences to encompass the meaning I had in mind, some creativity was needed to keep the rhythm flowing. At that, not every line is perfect, but I think you'll enjoy the ways in which these poems designed for entertainment and instruction also form a type of "music" of their own. As the old joke goes, at times it feels like you have to put the emPHAsis on the wrong sylLAble, but it all generally seems to come out right in the end.

CONTENTS

WRITERS, CLINICIANS, AND LEADERS

1. Arnold Sherman

Your artistry grows and you're learnin',
With heart and true feeling determined.
You're on a glad quest –
Music at its best –
The *best* of the best – Arnold Sherman.

2. Cathy Moklebust

If it rings in your heart then you know it's just
Music of quality you can trust.
Many tunes I recall
And I just love them all.
It's so beautiful, music by Moklebust.

3. Hart Morris

His music's a magic gift for us
To ring in a beautiful chorus.
Magician with rhythm,
We shine ringing with him.
And truly we're grateful, Hart Morris.

4. Tim Waugh

The best teaching you ever saw,
Musicianship worthy of awe,
A friend with great heart,
Treasure to our art –
The incomparable Mr. Tim Waugh!

5. Jason Wells

The man who gave us Ring of Fire
Is someone whose heart and desire
Lead us to be better
In every endeavor.
Mr. Jason Wells truly inspires!

6. Donald Allured

Don was the Maestro! We can tell
There's no one who can hold a candle
To him, from the start
Father of our art,
Allured – Master of Handbells!

Donald Allured – 1922-2011

7-9. David Davidson

David Davidson – alone he stands,
Sets a standard that is truly grand.
Ring with him and you've grown
For the music has known
The touch of the master's hand.

Musicality was his first issue.
David Davidson, when we were with you,
You brought forth the call –
Excellence above all.
You're our mentor and friend and we miss you.

David Davidson's stay here on earth
Has ended in heavenly rebirth.
Though his absence we grieve,
We know that he leaves
A legacy of untold worth.

David Davidson – 1948-2009

ALL handbell musicians, whether they ever met Don Allured
and David Davidson personally or not, have been influenced
by their high standard of musicianship and uncompromising
devotion to the elevation of the art of handbells. These giants
on whose shoulders we stand are sorely missed.

10-11. Kevin McChesney

There was a director named Kevin
Who thought that rehearsals weren't heaven
When they started at 1
And played till all done,
But they fell apart at measure 7.

There's a guy that they all call McChesney
Who likes run-throughs. "Yes, but I guess we
Should play bit by bit,
Step by step to get it,
Our performance will then at its best be."

There's nothing wrong with playing a piece from beginning to end in rehearsal. After all, that's how we are going to present it in concert or worship. But the most efficient learning takes place when the group takes on manageable segments and masters the technique and musicianship of each. All of the starting and stopping can be frustrating for ringers, but keep your eye on the goal and realize that this is actually a much faster and more effective way to learn the music. Do full run-throughs in rehearsal, too. Just don't make that *all* that you do.

12. Mike Kastner

Clinician, co-founder of STEP,
A teacher and leader with pep,
Solo ringer – a master,
It's all Michael Kastner,
The best friend a person can get.

13-16. On Behalf Of Writers

There's no doubt your part can be stressful.
Of solutions there is a chest-ful.
"What was s/he thinking?"
Just beautiful ringing!
We write so that you'll be successful.

There is a solution, so use it!
It can be played, so don't abuse it!
At times, when you're sinking,
You say, "What's s/he thinking?"
S/he's thinking of beautiful music!

You feel your muscles getting tighter.
You want to start cursing the writer.
Your part is a poser,
But trust the composer.
In time, this will be a delighter.

Without much rehearsal there's danger
Of treating the notes like they're strangers.
With care it is vital
To *practice* the title
And do justice to the arranger.

Composers/Arrangers don't write to deliberately trip you up or to make things difficult just for the sake of being difficult. Why would they do that? That makes no sense. Clearly, they want you to enjoy and use their music, and they have every desire that you will be successful.

There's no question that music can have challenges, but don't be too quick to blame the writer when you can't play something perfectly the first time through. (Ironically, ringers who express anger and frustration with writers for creating something challenging are often the very same ringers who accuse the writers of wrongdoing when a piece "isn't challenging enough.")

In Limericks 23-33, we'll talk about the Nine (Plus One) Solutions to *every* technical problem found in a ringer's part. When these Solutions become part of your toolkit, statements like "What was s/he thinking?" and "Why would s/he write it that way?" are eradicated forever.

17. Reaching For The Top

Campanile, Sonos, Raleigh, Vivace,
Pikes Peak Ringers, Arsis, and Agape –
It's not competition,
Each has its edition
Of showing us what we can all be.

Comparisons of groups, especially top-flight groups that set out to reach the apex of handbell performance, are inevitable, I suppose, but they don't have much value. Nothing we do in handbells is a contest. When a group like the Raleigh Ringers or Sonos brings handbells to concert venues that have never experienced our instrument before, it's a step forward for all of us. When Pikes Peak Ringers won a contest for which the prize was to record a track with internationally renowned cellist Yo-Yo Ma, *we all won!*

18. Thank You!

Growth as a musician's a feature
I hope will continue through each year.
I've had much good fortune
In many opportun–
Ities to work with special teachers.

My heartfelt thanks are always due to Brad Peterson, Dr. Lynn Whitten, Dr. Charles Eakin, Charles Wolzein, Dave Filsinger, Robert Crowder, James Dejarnette, and the many colleagues in handbells and other walks of musical life that I have been blessed to work with. All of us in music owe this rewarding part of our lives to generous directors, colleagues, teachers, and mentors. Do them and yourself a favor and send a note of thanks to the special people who helped make music a joyful part of your life.

FAMOUS HANDBELL PIECES

19. Green Blade

For Christmastime I would advise it.
For Eastertime you can reprise it.
My group in the past
Has had a real blast.
Have fun with Now the Green Blade Riseth.

20. Amazing

I guess somehow we'll find a place.
You'd think there just wouldn't be space
For yet one more setting
But we keep on getting
Arrangements of Amazing Grace.

The current record for the largest number of handbell arrangements of the same tune belongs to the great hymn of the church, Amazing Grace.

21. One Of The First

The range of experience is m–
Ore a spectrum than it's a schism.
Now more in the middle
And less of a riddle,
Among the first hard ones was Prisms.

Handbell choirs ARE improving over time! When Dr. William Payn's wonderful classic original piece Prisms first came out, you belonged to an advanced elite if you could play it. Now, it is still a challenging piece, but *many* groups can play it beautifully. It's nice to know that all the work we're doing IS making us better!

(The above titles may be found at the Jeffers Handbell Supply website http://www.handbellworld.com.)

TECHNIQUES

22. Attend To Technique

For confidence and skill to peak
And best artistry, don't you sneak
Past the basics you need
For music to succeed.
Be sure that you know your technique.

23-33. Nine (Plus One) Solutions

Your part as written you doubt,
But nine solutions I tout:
Share, pass, weave, other hand,
Reassign, four-in-hand,
Keyboard order? New plan!
Duplicate bells – yes, you can!
Get more ringers – it's grand!
And no, you can't leave notes out!

Leaving a note out is *NOT* an option! There are NINE ways to get all the notes played confidently, comfortably, and musically…

Share A Bell

Some passages you shouldn't dare.
There's too much for one – be aware!
I know some ringers still
Have their bells in their will!
But sometimes the best bet's to share.

"These bells are 'mine.' I've put my bell assignment *in my will!* No one else will touch them till they pry them out of my cold, dead hands. No one else can play them and I have to MAKE this part work." I'm happy to say that this mentality, once very common, appears to be fading into the past. If you can't play your assigned notes musically and in a relaxed manner, one solution is to have a neighbor play one of "your" bells. (They'll give it back – probably. ☺)

Pass A Bell

You think that your part's getting mangled
But approach it from a new angle.
Pass a bell hand-to-hand;
This makes "can't" into "can"
And will get you out of a tangle.

Weave

You know you can't drop one or leave
A note out, but cheer up, believe!
This trick helps you stay
Out of your own way.
You *can* play that part – learn to weave!

EVERY ringer needs to know how to weave! Beginners should be taught weaving – it is *not* an "advanced" technique. There's no question it takes some practice, but it is essential that ringers know how to manipulate three bells with two hands smoothly and musically.

Start With The Other Hand

Before this passage you curse
You might think of it in reverse.
Maybe start the line with
Your other hand. Bliss!
You'll come out right as you rehearse.

Starting a phrase or small segment with the "wrong" hand is a simple solution to many logistical problems. Of course, you really started with the "correct" hand if the music is played well.

Reassign A Bell

It's "your bell," but you can't seem to line it
Up with the music, even find it.
You may need a hand
From someone who can –
You may need to just reassign it.

If you can't play a bell effectively and neither of your neighbors has a hand free, maybe the bell can be reassigned to someone down the table who can play that bell for this piece.

Four-In-Hand

If the part's tough and handbells are small,
It may be that you should recall
A way to put two
In one hand, then you
Split them up again. You played it all!

Four-in-hand is a good solution to get out of a logistical tangle when the bells are small enough to put two in one hand. Remember that this is a temporary situation. Once the rough spot is managed, take the pair apart again.

Change From Keyboard Order

You try to make sense from disorder.
Of an answer you're right on the border.
Take your bell and reset it
To where you can get it.
For now, depart from keyboard order.

If your part says to ring G4, then G#4, then A4, one option is to set the G#4 to the right of where it normally rests, still in the upper "black keys" row, but to the right of A4 (A#4's area). You ring G4 with your left hand, G#4 with your right hand (it's now within easy reach), and A4 with your left hand (this bell is also just under your hand and simple to grab). This only works under conditions where it causes no technical or musical problems to move the bell out of order, to adjust in the next few bars because A4 is now in the "wrong" (non-"home") hand, or to reset to keyboard order after this passage.

Duplicate Bell

When the music is taking a beating,
The solution is not note-deleting.
Some notes you assign
To someone down the line.
Use a duplicate bell, it's not cheating!

Notice that this limerick says you assign certain "notes" to someone else along the table, not certain bells. You may well be able to ring a bell musically and comfortably for most of the piece. But there are a couple of times when it just isn't going to work using the other solutions we've discussed. Grab a duplicate bell from another set and give that to a ringer who can play the note effectively at those points. It's rare that a handbell choir is the only game in town. Most programs function in a region where there are other bell sets available, owned by people who are happy to make a loan for a specific situation.

Many Hands Make Light Work

"Many hands make light work," it is said.
If parts are tough you may feel led
To bring in more ringers.
The real humdinger
Is that it works! Hope is not dead!

Not every program has the luxury of having extra ringers immediately available, but most of us *can* recruit extra hands for a piece or two when needed – from the sub list, vocal choir, youth group, local high school, and so on. If a piece requires 14, 16, 19, 23 ringers to be played in a way that communicates the music well, get the extra ringers needed. Pikes Peak Ringers generally uses 14 ringers to play 5 octaves plus three bass notes in the 2's. But sometimes we've used 15, 16, or even 17 ringers on a piece if that's what's required to play confidently and musically.

Comments On The "Nine Solutions."

First, if you ever find yourself crossing arms or throwing a bell down to grab another bell quickly with the same hand, that's wrong, and it's ALWAYS wrong! If you find you are doing one of these improper techniques, you have nine effective solutions available to you.

Second, writers are often accused of not knowing how to ring or not understanding the techniques involved in playing their music. There's no question that there are passages in handbell pieces that might have been written another way and perhaps that other way would have been simpler. Still, writers are primarily concerned with the sound that is made in performance. The responsibility for making that sound rests with the director and ringers, and they have a toolkit of nine devices that make ALL bell music playable in a way that communicates. So, ringers and directors, I encourage you to give your poor writers the benefit of the doubt; with so many effective tools at your disposal, playing the music artistically and in a relaxed and confident way is up to you!

The "Plus One" (Tenth) Solution

If you're not up to this piece just now
And feel it won't fly true and proud,
There's no shame; you find
A piece of simpler kind.
Confident ringing's your vow.

The Nine Solutions are *always* enough to get you through a given technical entanglement. Still, they take practice. You may simply not have the experience to apply these techniques to the music at this time. The clock at bell rehearsals is always ticking – loudly! – so if you find there just isn't time to work through one of the solutions and still produce fine music when the deadline comes, set this piece aside for another time and play something that you can manage and feel confident about at your current level. There is **NEVER** anything wrong with playing something simpler and doing it really well!!

34-35. LV

LV is a beautiful kind
Of sound when given its time.
Four symbols send
LV to an end –
Change technique, LV, R, target sign.

LV is a beautiful kind
Of sound when given its time.
Two symbols *don't* send
LV to an end –
LV sounds through rests and barlines.

LV doesn't end at the next barline. If there's an LV in measure 1 and no new LV, R, change of technique (like to malleting the bells on the table, TD, martellato, and so on), or "target sign" (as far as I know, that symbol is properly called a "damp sign") until measure 38, then the bells aren't damped for 37 measures.

LV also sustains right through rests. This begs the question "Why are the rests there, then?" That's fair, from a certain point of view, because rests usually tell ringers to take a physical action which is to damp. The reason you'll see an LV that sounds through the rests is that it is cleaner to have the rests on the page than a lot of ties. The rests can also be an aid to keeping track of the counting.

36-38. Ringing Circles And Shakes

The sound of a bell from the side
Of the casting is made, so you glide
In a circle. Don't bend
Your wrist, or tip end.
It's healthier and grace provides.

When ringing a bell move your arm
For more than beauty and charm.
When playing a shake,
A circle still make
So it won't sound "hard" like an alarm.

You ring in an upward round shape
Creating a lovely soundscape.
Now, make no mistake,
When you get to a shake,
If making a circle…you're great!

Shakes are executed using the same ringing circle as regular
ringing. The tendency is to "park" a shake, but the sound of a
bell comes from the side of the casting in every direction. This
is why we make ringing circles. True, it's because it looks
nice, but it's also so that the side of the bell moves through as
much physical space as possible, giving a fuller, richer sound.
For the same reasons, a shake needs to move through the same
arc as regular ringing, looking better and producing a more
pleasing sound.

39. Bass Bells

You have to be specially gifted.
The strong from the weak will be sifted.
To ring a bass bell
It's not hard to tell –
You have to be able to lift it.

This limerick is tongue-in-cheek, of course. Nevertheless, I often see bass bells being played by people who are physically incapable of lifting them in a healthy, relaxed way. The art of handbells shows a type of favoritism when it comes to bass bells in the sense that these bells are more easily lifted and played by people who are taller and have stronger arms. That may seem unfair, but no more so than basketball being a game played primarily by tall people. Handbells is also a somewhat archaically sexist activity in the sense that it's simply a fact of life that more men are physically able to manipulate the big bells than women. That said, one of the best bass bell ringers I've ever known is a woman, so there it is. ☺

40-41. Watch!

You don't want your ringing to botch.
You want to be truly top-notch.
For the count, feel, and more,
Lift your head from the score.
The director can help you, so watch!

Much more than a "music inspector,"
(S)he's there to be help and protector.
(S)he keeps you together,
Helps you look and sound better,
So look up and watch the director.

Watching the director as you ring is *NOT* optional. It is also not necessarily easy to do, but there are specific methods that help ringers learn exactly HOW to watch, WHEN to watch, and WHAT to watch for. I've written an article called "How to be the Ultimate Massed Ringing Participant" which covers a variety of subjects related to rehearsals and preparing music, and the first part of it is devoted to learning how to watch the director (in all contexts, not just massed ringing).

The article is FREE at http://www.sonologymusic.com (click "Articles").

42-45. Don't Count On It!

When watching directors, don't count!
For tempo, they are the fount.
That voice in your head
Has no light to shed.
This obstacle you can surmount!

When the tempo takes off at a run
Like a bullet that's shot from a gun,
Let the leader hold sway.
It might save the day.
There's a chance that you may end as one.

When your ringing just isn't together,
You don't think the storm you can weather,
"Don't count!" is the rule,
"Move when I move!" the tool.
The burden gets light as a feather.

When watching directors, just ring.
Just move when they move, that's the thing.
Counting's in the way;
Move with him/her, I say.
This will make your musicianship sing!

I can see faces fall and sometimes even hear groans when I instruct ringers in festivals and workshops not to count. Every director in the room clutches his/her brow and says, "Oh, dear God, he just told them *not to count!*"

Counting is not a bad thing by any means and is a necessary tool to learn how to read music and how to participate in the rhythmic nature of the bell choir. It is a means to becoming familiar with and internalizing the music you are learning. But there is a time to count and a time not to count, and it is surprising how soon in the learning process ringers should get *away* from counting. If that little guy in your head who is counting the music is counting the least bit differently from the director, you are not going to be with him/her or the rest of the group.

I've seen hundreds of ringers get very frustrated with themselves and the music and ringing in general because they *know* they are counting and are working very hard at doing it correctly, but they just can't seem to keep up or be with everyone else. Truth is, the problem is very likely the counting itself. I repeat – counting is a *tool* to learn the music in the early stages. Counting is not a goal in and of itself. The goal is to internalize the music, feel the rhythm and the phrasing, and play *without* consciously counting. Watch the director, don't count yourself, and ring your bell when the director moves. Let the director do the counting. That way, one person is counting and everyone is with him/her instead of 13 people all counting to themselves, many or all of whom may be counting differently from the leader.

So don't count! Well, count to get familiar with your part, but challenge yourself to *stop* counting as early in the game as possible. Replace counting with moving as the director moves. It works! Miracles happen!

46-47. Martellato

When executing a mart,
Put "two tacos high" on your chart –
Tacos on their side,
Not on end or up high,
No more than two inches to start.

When executing a mart,
Be gentle right from the start.
Don't start from great heights.
Heaven's sake, keep it light!
This is music, not a martial art!

Want your choir's martellatos to be together? It's as simple as this: have everyone start the martellato from just a couple inches off the pad, regardless of the size of their bell. Everyone starts from "two tacos high." (This is a strange catch-phrase, but it seems to work, so go with me here. ☺) This way, everyone executes the technique through a small bit of space and everyone's space should be roughly equal so differences in ringers' heights won't affect martellato.

Also, martellato is a *very* loud sound. There is no sound that we make in bells that is louder, short of dropping the bells on the floor. ☺ It doesn't take a lot of effort or weight. Martellato is a light technique, quick, with very little power.

If all ringers do those two things – start from "two tacos high" ("two hockey pucks high" for our Canadian friends ☺) and play lightly with little effort – martellatos will be played together in a controlled way. In fact, since little distance is needed and the bells are well away from ringers' faces, it is also *required* that ringers watch the director when playing martellatos!

48. Malleting

To mallet and do it quite well,
Think of drawing sound *out* of the bell.
The stroke that goes down
Should be less, the rebound
Is bigger – that's how you can tell.

Malleting with bells on the table is also a very light technique taking little effort. Wrists and forearms should be relaxed. If you want it louder, give the stroke a bit more speed, don't worry about giving it more weight or muscle.

49. Plucking Low Bells

Ok, so how do you pluck
The low bells? Reach in, don't get stuck.
The clapper you lift
Then throw down – just a bit –
Not much force and you've done it! Good luck!

50. Plucking High Bells

When plucking high bells there's no space
To reach a hand in and get placed.
If there's time, give the clapper
A bit of a tapper;
If there's not, flip it toward the bell-face.

With bigger bells, about C5 and below, there is room to reach a hand in and "throw" the clapper lightly to pluck. With smaller bells, there simply isn't room for that, so either tap the clapper lightly or flip it up toward you. Flipping the clapper toward the bell-face (the bell symbol on the handle) runs the risk of getting a double sound as the clapper strikes the casting on the side nearest you, then falls and strikes the side resting on the pad. This is why you don't use flipping with bigger bells. But with smaller bells, the double strike is unlikely, and the "feel" of this technique is easy to control with some practice.

51. Staccato, No Performance Note Or Other Symbol

There are options when notes are staccato,
No letters appear with the dot. O,
Bells with mallets are struck,
Choose to thumb damp or pluck
Or even use light martellato.

Sometimes no specific indication is given for how to execute staccato notes. Most writers are comfortable with having the director and ringers choose from the several options for creating staccato sounds. So you decide what is most musically and technically effective at these points. As long as all ringers do the same technique (or perhaps treble does one technique and bass another, depending on the musical situation), you're good to go.

52-53. Weaving

Only two hands have you received,
But at times you must ring bells in threes.
Your arms should not cross.
No bells should be tossed.
No tangled web should you weave.

The main purpose here, I would say,
Is to get right out of your own way.
Ring each to its side;
Step with it, even wide.
On the table each in place you lay.

ALL ringers need to know how to weave. The technique is not terribly complex, but is better learned by having someone show you than through reading about it, so I won't attempt a description here. But if you haven't learned how to weave in a relaxed, confident way, be sure to get with someone who can teach you.

I'll reiterate the note from our discussion of the Nine Solutions for addressing technical challenges (Limericks 23-33): if you ever find yourself crossing arms or throwing a bell down to grab another bell quickly with the same hand, that's wrong, and it's ALWAYS wrong! Weaving is one of the Nine Solutions; it takes some practice, to be sure, but ALL ringers need to master this vital technique.

54-56. Mistakes

It's a mistake! Yep, you made one.
I'm afraid it just can't be undone.
It was just a hiccup;
Don't beat yourself up.
Hey, come on – ringing's s'posed to be fun!

A mistake! Oh, no! Did it happen?
But that's past. You need to tap in -
To the here-and-now flow,
So just let it go.
It's over, so get your mind back in.

Your ringing's been going just great,
But goofs happen – there's no debate.
Don't despair. Make a choice
To keep calm. Heed the voice
That says "Better never than late."

Better to leave a note out than to play a "right" note late. This
is NOT to say that leaving out notes deliberately is acceptable
(see the section on the Nine Solutions to technical tangles,
Limericks 23-33)!! The point here is that missing a note is a
more acceptable mistake in performance than playing the note
late. The moment containing the missed note has passed. Find
where everyone is and join in as soon as you can.

57-58. Catch And Release

Mistakes can make you feel tense
Because they seem harsh and immense.
Your mistake you can own,
But it's passed now. Go on!
Yes, "catch and release" makes good sense.

You may have taken a vow:
"No mistakes!" But be here and now.
Just catch and release!
You'll be more at ease,
Make less goofs the more you allow.

A true paradox in performing music of any kind, including playing handbells, is that the more you simply allow yourself to make mistakes, the less mistakes you will make. "Catch and release" is a term used in fishing, where you catch a fish and then let it go either because it is too small or because of rules concerning quotas and conservation. The principle is pure gold in handbell ringing. One of the worst effects a mistake can have is to cause more trouble and more mistakes because you are upset about the first one and still feel uptight about it. Making music is a very "present tense" activity. Be "now, here" or you may be "nowhere." "Catch" the mistake, acknowledge that you made it, allow it to happen. Then "release" it. It's in the past, and we're playing *this* measure now, not that one. This is a VERY effective method for reducing the number of mistakes you make!

RINGERS, DIRECTORS, AND THE HANDBELL PROGRAM

59. Be On Time!

It's respectful, it's courteous and kind
To keep others' schedules in mind.
They work hard to get in
When rehearsal begins.
You *know* when we start! Be on time!

60. Turn It Off!

We like to hear every handbell's tone
And know when the music is well done.
Other sounds interrupt
And can really disrupt.
In rehearsal, please turn off your cell phone!

Pet peeve of mine! Please? For me? ☺

61. Subs

Who cares if they're young or they're old?
You'd rather be left in the cold?
If they know sightreading
And are eager to ring
Then they're hired. A good sub is gold!

If one regular ringer is missing from rehearsal, we go ahead. If two are missing, we can get by this once, doing mostly technical work, but if we know two are missing again next week, we're likely to cancel or reschedule. If three are missing, we go home. This is true even if we have great subs. You have to rehearse the music on the instrument that is going to perform it, and that's your original A team.

Of course, keep a list of reliable subs going at all times to cover when one (or two) regular ringers are absent. A sub will miss notes, of course, maybe even quite a few, but better to have a part at 50% than at 0%.

Important Note: It's not always possible to get a sub. When a part is vacant with no sub, the neighboring ringers *DO NOT* try to cover those bells!!!! God gave each of us only two hands, and there are limits to how many bells those two hands can play musically. Do the math: if the ringer that's at this rehearsal plays only his/her own part, we have one part being played well and another part being left out. If that same ringer tries to get those other bells, the ones assigned to the ringer who's absent this week, we have *two* parts being played very badly and we're MUCH worse off!! I've been known to physically remove bells from the table to keep ringers from trying to play the bells that aren't covered at this rehearsal. This rule goes for all choirs and ringers, regardless of experience and talent. It doesn't matter how terrific a ringer you are, there are limits to what you can play. The disease of "Oh-I-can-get-it-itis" is one of the strongest reasons for keeping a good sub list and using subs consistently.

62-63. Oh! (Page Turns)

At first, I thought it was age.
With me they would all get enraged.
But I figured out why
Those notes went right by:
Would somebody please turn my page?!

Each ringer in this day and age yearns
For when some scholar or sage earns
Respect, cheers, and hollers,
Our thanks and big dollars
For finding a way to do page turns.

There's only ***one*** method for turning pages that works: memorize something and turn early. Ringers sometimes ask if they can memorize something over the page and turn late, but I believe anything done late in bells is dangerous. You *have* to be physically reaching for the page several bars before the end of that page. Until someone invents a foot pedal for turning our pages or we are all reading from scrolling computer screens, this is it!

64-66. Make The Group A Priority

We all have a lot on our plates.
Life is busy and fast and that's great.
Discuss with authority –
Bells are a priority.
Agree WELL ahead on your dates!

Make sure your commitment is strong.
Take care as you go along.
The group's a priority
Because the majority
Is needed to play every song.

It takes time to make music fine,
To be in this group, make it shine.
Most people's schedules
Sadly are just dreadful.
Commit ONLY if you have time.

Being in a bell choir takes a commitment of time, pure and simple. Even more simply, rehearsing a piece of music requires minutes – hours – with bells in your hands. Participation in a handbell choir *IS* more demanding than being in other musical organizations. That may not be "fair," but it's what we've signed on for.

The number one addiction in the world, far surpassing alcohol, smoking, drugs, and whatever the media is letting us know about this week, is **being busy**. The vast majority of people feel they can take on more than they realistically can. We take on more and more, never dropping anything to make room. And most people's lives are at best frantic blurs that they don't really get to experience, and at worst unhealthy, painful, insane rides that are keeping them from the joys of family, friends, and being the wonderful people God created them to be.

If the time involved in being at rehearsals, services, performances, and in helping with the extra-musical logistics of the group is just too much, sad to say the best alternative for all concerned is to step down. Have a full complement of devoted ringers who can make the time work, even if that means ringing 3 octaves instead of 4 or 5 this year. Remember that if you own 5 octaves, you also own 3, or 2, or even 1 (yes, there is fine music available for four ringers playing one octave).

Way too many programs suffer from absences and having to shuffle players around. I intend no disrespect for the fact that some people choose to live very busy lives and are happy having made that choice. My experience is that the overwhelming majority of people who have completely packed schedules are not happy, and are in fact miserable or at best oblivious to what they are doing to themselves and others. While I would love to preach my sermon on reducing the frenetic pace of life so that people have the chance to live peaceful, happy, fulfilling lives to the entire world, in this small volume I'll settle for making the point that the handbell choir requires *a strong commitment of time*.

We volunteer for this organization, so of course it goes in the cracks left between family, work, trips, and so on. Please be sure to carefully evaluate just how small those cracks are in your life so that when you sign on to ring you are giving the time necessary for a successful program. And please re-evaluate these matters often, because every indication is that life will only get busier as time goes on.

67. Faster!

You follow tempos to the letter,
But some ringers are real go-getters.
They might do your bidding,
But who are we kidding?
We all know that faster is better!

(Joke!)

68. Too Fast – It's OK!

You stand and stare, looking aghast!
The director is going so fast!
Just think, "soft and light."
Get what you *can* right.
Trust yourself that you'll get it at last.

69-70. Faster Sounds Loud

Fast tempos make volume more; play
With less force and not with more. Hey,
Less time, more within it
Means more notes per minute,
So play *light* for "fast" and "forte."

Fast music already sounds loud
With notes in a furious cloud
Of sound. Fast and thick
Means to be *light* and quick.
Less force does "loud and fast" proud.

To play fast music, ring the bells as if they were light in your hands, never heavy and loud (except for very rare musical effects). Speed already sounds loud because more notes are sounding in a given period of time. So there's no need to play forcefully to try to get volume. Rather, play lightly with a relaxed, swift stroke that isn't punched.

71-75. Not Much To Do

Sometimes I hear ringers declare
That their parts are just barely there.
You have less to do,
But it's still up to you
To make all your listeners care.

Your part may seem boring, it's true,
And it's hard when there's not much to do,
But as handbells you lift
Know your music's a gift.
Let your love for the music shine through.

When you have so few notes in the score
And ringing this piece "is a bore,"
It's well worth your while
To work on your style,
So make how you LOOK count for more.

When faced with a part that's uneven
With not much to do, feels like leavin's
A choice: don't you dare!
MAKE it fun and take care –
It'll work out if you keep believin'.

Sometimes you know from the start
There's not much to do in this part.
Anyone can be busy,
Ring bells till they're dizzy.
To make your part sing – that takes heart.

I know, I know! "This piece is so BORING!" Actually, the *piece* isn't boring, *your part* is just not as active and engaging as *you'd* like it to be. It's been well-said that "There are no boring parts, only boring ringers." Remember that handbell music is written to communicate and touch the listener, not to babysit ringers. All parts have to be played, the interesting ones AND the dull ones.

The individual ringer's job in *every* piece is to be a part of the whole. This is true of highly challenging parts as your job is to play those parts confidently so that listeners and watchers aren't aware of the technical obstacles you have overcome. The same is true when it's your turn to cover the less-than-exciting part. If the technical challenges are few or non-existent, rather than succumb to eye-rolling and deep sighs of dissatisfaction, embrace the opportunity to develop your artistry and to succeed as a strong musician, to communicate the musical whole in a beautiful and exciting way.

Technical challenge is only one level in handbell music, and the most basic level at that. In fact, it is the element of the music that should be completely invisible and inaudible to those to whom we present our music. Next is musicianship – play the less-technically-engaging part as a seamless and expressive part of the musical whole. There is also the visual aspect of ringing; a "boring" part should never *appear* "boring" to those watching. The movement of ringing gives you endless opportunities to enhance the musical whole, regardless of how simple the part may be to play.

You've mastered the technical, musical, and visual elements and you're still "bored?" How about memorizing your part? This isn't just to amuse yourself. It's an effective and important way to create sight lines with your congregation or audience and to allow your face to communicate the music (something that should be happening regardless of whether you've memorized your part or not, but that is certainly enhanced when you have).

In Pikes Peak Ringers, the most extreme example of this problem that we've encountered was a piece where the CD4 part literally played six times in the entire arrangement. Arguably, we could have rung the piece with one less ringer and simply reassigned those notes (in another piece with a similar situation we did just that, but that can be a dangerous solution – more on that later). But, believe it or not, those six notes just could not be reassigned in a smooth, musical manner.

I bring up this example to illustrate the hard and fast, never-to-be-tampered-with rule about assigning, which is:

Bells are assigned in ways that they can be played confidently and musically.

The companion rule, equally inviolable, is:

Even a single bell that can't be played confidently and musically at even a single point MUST be reassigned.

(Use of duplicates is encompassed in this rule. You aren't physically reassigning an individual bell, but when you use a duplicate you are reassigning a note to another ringer.)

So in the above instance, we needed the proper number of hands to play the piece effectively and, sure enough, one ringer was required to play a whopping six notes in this piece.

Boring? Sure. But necessary. So my ringer's challenge clearly wasn't the technical demands of the part, it was how to make her assignment an expressive contribution to the musical whole through good phrasing, use of movement including posture and attitude during the long segments when she had nothing to do, and even memorizing the part, which certainly wasn't a daunting task in this case.

Pikes Peak Ringers is noted for a strong visual style of ringing. This ringer met the situation with fortitude and managed to find ways to move alongside the ringers who did have notes to play so that she blended in beautifully. She used the back-to-front motion and other stances that PPR uses in a manner which said, "I could ring at any time." That may sound a little silly and perhaps artificial, but maintaining body language and facial expressions that indicate that you are very much a part of the music is appropriate. After all, you want those listening and watching to be moved by the music. You *don't* want to "advertise" that a ringer just doesn't have a lot of notes to play.

76-78. Bell Hogs

An experienced ringer can bring
Many assets to music we ring,
But we don't keep score
And see who rings more.
To be a "bell hog's" not the thing!

It's tempting to say "Bring it on!
I can play more and more, on and on!"
You've got two hands – good!
Take on more than you should
And the *whole choir's* hard work is gone!

To be a bell hog brings no joy
To the group and we must avoid
All ringers who wanna
Show-off. Prima donnas
Will truly our music destroy.

"Kevin, why did you call the method of reassigning a simple part using one less ringer 'dangerous?'" Eliminating one standard part – in the case previously described, the CD4 part – and assigning those notes to neighbors and others with hands free can work well ONLY if the reassigned notes can be played confidently and musically, every single one of them, no exceptions! The "danger" lies in overestimating the ability of ringers to cover extra bells. Maybe it can be done well, but the likelihood is that it will cross over into "bell hog" territory, and **_nothing_** destroys the musicianship, artistry, confidence, communication, visual presentation, and even the basic technical flow of a bell choir more completely and tragically than having a "bell hog" (or worse, more than one).

Give the listeners and watchers a group in which the "boring" parts are played with style, emotion, clarity, and confidence! Don't give them the *chance* to react with "That one ringer sure seemed to have a lot to do," or "I sometimes wondered if Sarah was going to make it through," or "I wonder why Jennifer was scrambling around so much while other ringers were just standing there," or "Boy, that one guy sure stands out; he's all over the place," or anything even remotely like it. If we're doing our jobs as ringers and directors properly, we should *never* hear these kinds of comments – not even once! What we do is about music – it is NOT about how many bells a ringer can play!

Read on for more on this important subject…

79-82. Choosing Music

The bell choir succeeds – it can't lose! –
When confident and not confused.
Find music they'll manage,
That's to their advantage.
Success relies on songs you choose.

Will music come out good or bad?
The answer makes some people mad.
Choose music (don't laugh!)
For the number you *have*,
Not the number that you *wish* you had!

Choose music by number of hands
That make up your sweet little band,
Not by bells in your set.
For success, don't forget
Choose music that says "Yes, we can!"

Let's say that of octaves you've five
But you're short ringers. Yes, you'll survive!
If there's five, there's three or
There's two, one, or four.
The right songs keep programs alive!

I've had directors tell me, too many times for comfort, things
like "We have one young gal who's so good she plays our
entire top octave," or "Our bass ringer is amazing; he plays all
the 3's himself," or "We play five octaves with only nine
ringers," or "We lost three ringers this year but we still ring all
the bells." The honest response would be "Well, you don't do
it very well." They say these things with such pride, so out of
compassion and in the interest of good teaching I respond as
gently as I can, but my message is essentially to encourage
people to examine these musically destructive situations.

Few teachers in handbells have encountered as many advanced, phenomenally gifted ringers as I have, and I can tell you that *not one* of them can play even two adjacent parts (like the all-too-common combination of GA6 and B6C7) effectively and *musically* on every piece. In specific instances, it may work. But refer again to our rules of assigning:

Bells are assigned in ways that they can be played confidently and musically.

Even a single bell that can't be played confidently and musically at even a single point MUST be reassigned.

I realize conquering a part that involves numerous bells can be rewarding and fun, and there's nothing wrong with that as long as the part *is being played confidently and musically*. God gave us only two hands. There ARE limits to what an individual ringer, even the finest ringer in the world, can play. The most advanced ringers I've encountered qualify as the most advanced ringers partly *because* they understand their limitations and are willing and eager to find technical solutions that bring about the finest musical presentation.

"But we only have nine ringers." Then don't play all five octaves. Play what nine ringers can play confidently and musically.[1]

---

[1] 2-3 octave music is a good choice for nine ringers. The central two octaves, G4 to G6, are played by eight ringers. The G6 ringer also plays A6, and the ninth ringer plays B6C7. Notes below G4 may be added *only* when they can be played properly; this will happen occasionally, but many of these optional notes will *not* be rung.

Ringing musically and confidently is ringing in ways that are not distracting to those listening and watching, with no stress and no scrambling and no tension. I don't care how good that guy ringing the entire bass by himself is – he *can't* be doing it musically.

If you don't have enough hands to ring all the bells you are trying to ring, ring less bells! As I've mentioned, if you own five octaves, you own four, three, two, even one. There is music written to be expressive and exciting for bell sets of all sizes (even one octave/four ringers). It is ALWAYS better to present something confidently and musically than it is to take on more bells simply for the sake of taking on more bells.

Inappropriate assignments and "bell hog" syndrome utterly *destroy* our music! They are completely unnecessary, given the many options that we have available to us for assigning and for choosing music.

83. Gloves

From the time you first heard them, you loved
Handbells' sound, as if sent from above.
Both the sound and the sight
Should be polished and bright
So always take care to wear gloves.

Actually, we wear gloves to protect our hands when ringing,
but it's a nice side-effect that we also keep our instrument
beautiful to look at as well as to listen to.

84-85. Neighbor

You made a mistake 'midst your labors,
But errors you musn't belabor.
Should you take the blame
For something so lame?
Just frown and look mad at your neighbor.

Another mistake 'midst your labors
Gives pain as sharp as a saber.
But should you take credit
As music you edit?
Look fed up and point at your neighbor.

(Joke!)

86. Call An Extra Rehearsal

It shouldn't be too controversial.
If playing a wedding, commercial,
Concert, morning show,
Festival, then you know
You might need an extra rehearsal.

Simple math: if there's more music to accomplish and the goal is always to play confidently and artistically, you need more rehearsal time. Of course, there are limits to how much music even the most advanced group can play effectively, so...

87. Do Less And Do It Well

You know it isn't a contest
To see who can play the most. Stress
And tension dispel –
Do less, do it well.
With less pressure you'll play your best.

While this ditty applies to the evils of "bell hog" syndrome that I've previously addressed, it also points out a malady that way too many choirs suffer from – taking on more music in their program than they are able to present well. If you feel "under the gun" because you always seem to be pressing hard to get ready for the next presentation in worship or concert, it's likely that you are trying to play too much music. There is **_NEVER_** anything wrong with doing less and doing it well. After all, the goal is to communicate through the music in a way that sets the listeners apart and gives them a relaxed, peaceful space to absorb the emotion and message of what you are playing. They can't do this if you are "just getting through," performing in an unprepared way and experiencing a lot of nervousness and anxiety about your ringing. It's not fun for you and it can't reach the listeners. It's better to take on a more reasonable amount of work. There's great fulfillment to be found in knowing you are hitting every title out of the park, and the only way to do that is to be sure you have ample rehearsal time to prepare and polish your music.

88-89. Are We Ready?

There comes a time when you are ready.
Feeling confident, ringing is heady.
When confidence shows,
It's then you can know
Your ringing is solid and steady.

Ready to share with your bells?
Confidence is how you tell.
Overwhelmed, scared, and such?
Then don't do so much!
Remember, do less, do it well!

The adage "Do less and do it well!" would serve many bell choirs well, regardless of experience level. Above all other considerations, instilling *confidence* is the primary purpose of rehearsals. If the group has not felt confident in its presentations in worship or concerts, it's time to look at scaling back. Music can be communicated effectively only when the group is well-prepared, and "well-prepared" is defined as being confident about what you are doing technically and musically. Some of our finest concert groups like Vivace, Sonos, and Pikes Peak Ringers communicate music wonderfully – and one of the main reasons for that is that they are confident. They know the music well and feel strong in performing it.

But this principle isn't all about experience level. In February of 1993, I saw and heard a performance by a "Mother's Morning Out" group of 7 or 8 ladies who had all started ringing the previous September. They played a 2-octave Level 1+ piece, no bell changes, no techniques beyond ringing and LV, and they played it elegantly and with a sincere heart for the beautiful music. They were confident about playing, and it was obvious that they enjoyed sharing this lovely music with others. My point? After all these years, I still remember that performance, don't I? The lesson is clear: the group didn't have to be playing complex music to make a lasting impression.

90-91. More Than Notes

Whenever you hear someone mention
"Be true to the music's intention" –
Dynamics and such!
Expression does much.
Make the tune of your heart an extension.

Music's not routine and not rote.
Dynamics would get my strong vote
As a vital first step
To give life and pep.
When ringing play more than the notes.

92. Musicianship

Concentrate on your musicianship,
Don't have your mind on your last fishin' trip.
(A confession from me:
Just wanted to see
If I'd find a rhyme for "musicianship.") ☺

93. Tune Bondage

We love a good tune that is catchy,
But sanity gets mighty patchy
When "tune bondage" stays
Through the week, every day.
Please don't end the rehearsal with that piece!

Ever have a tune stuck in your head for days because you
ended rehearsal with it? That's part of what we signed on for.
It's good for you. ☺

94. Be Positive

Directors – you follow their lead.
For encouragement they have a need.
Who wants to hear grumbling,
Complaints that you're mumbling?
Be positive in word and deed.

Clearly, no one can be absolutely positive and upbeat all the time. Still, my experience has been that there are some ringers who are determined to be negative at every turn. Even a small attempt at being positive attracts a great deal of positive energy to the rehearsal room. We want to be a positive influence in the lives of the people we ring for. It starts with encouraging and being a positive influence for your director and for each other. Positive spirit attracts more positive spirit. It's as simple and as wonderful as that.

95. Conflict

Bell choirs are music team-style,
So conflicts you must reconcile.
It just feeds a fight
To "always be right."
Admit you're wrong once in a while.

I had to learn the hard way that it's often much more
important to be happy than to be right. My prayer for you is
that you come to realize this vital principle for dealing with
the unavoidable conflicts and concerns in your bell choir
program naturally and considerately.

96. Work It Out

A ringer whose label seems "jerk?"
Someone who won't esteem work?
You'd best have a talk,
Find a way, walk the walk.
Handbells is clearly teamwork.

97. Don't Complain, Don't Explain

The tendency is to complain
And every mistake to explain.
Those around you may moan.
They've got "stuff" of their own.
Don't complain or explain – it's a pain!

The "Don't Complain, Don't Explain" policy is highly effective for making rehearsals more efficient and more pleasant, especially in the early stages of learning. The need to limit complaining is obvious. Beyond that, some ringers feel the need to explain to everyone around them why they made a mistake – EVERY time! Frankly, while fellow ringers and the director care about you as a person and fellow musician, they are not interested in why you make every mistake. They have obstacles of their own that they are dealing with. Explaining every mistake is at worst self-centered and at best something that holds up rehearsals terribly. Learn from your mistakes, grow in each stage of learning the music, but leave others free to do the same.

98-101. Effective Practice

Don't just run through beginning to end.
That's important, but better to lend
A hand to each section.
Give details direction
To get the results you intend.

It's great fun to ring a full run-through,
But remember as each piece we come to
To focus on small
Sections, phrases, and all
Of the details will make the whole come through.

There's no more efficient rehearsal
Than one that includes the dispersal
Of troubles through handling
Small chunks; understanding
Details makes success universal.

"We made it beginning to end!
It's time to play for our friends!"
No, it's not! In our art
A run-through's just the *start*.
It's now that our best work *begins!*

From these poems on practicing, it would appear that I believe in never doing full run-throughs in rehearsal, and nothing could be further from the truth. Playing a piece from beginning to end at various stages in its development is vital for internalizing the music and to instill confidence in ringers. But the most effective rehearsal method is to break a piece down into manageable chunks, working out technical problems and giving detailed direction on musical elements. Then we put these portions together, creating larger and larger sections that are "under our belts," until we feel strong about the piece as a whole and know that we are communicating confidently. Sometimes, this kind of rehearsing seems sluggish to ringers, but it's actually much quicker and more efficient than just doing run-throughs over and over.

The opposite – splitting the piece into fragments that are really too small to understand musically and continuing to do that without putting larger portions together – is also not effective rehearsal. So a balance needs to be reached.

102-103. Joy In The Journey

Repeating can bore or annoy.
Do it again? Well, oh, boy!
Rehearsing is fun,
Learning all bars or one.
The process itself is a joy.

Mastered your part? You're just one.
Others still learn and aren't done.
Don't call an attorney!
There's joy in the journey!
Remind yourself – ringing is fun!

It's been beautifully said that "There are no boring parts, only boring ringers." If you feel you've got your part down and wish the rest of the group would just get on with it, remember that there is always something more you can bring to the music – finesse, phrasing, visual style, memorization. We spend the majority of our musical time rehearsing, so remember to take pleasure in the journey.

104. Ask For Their Best

Before you, a musical task
They haven't made work in the past.
They will understand
If you teach, give a hand.
They'll do it, but you have to ask!

Directors sometimes get frustrated that results haven't come about. My first question is usually, "Did you *ask* them to do it?" Amazingly, the answer commonly boils down to "No." Ringers *are* on the director's side and want to do well. They want to learn and are willing to try what you have in mind. Don't be shy about asking for more, teaching them new things, stretching them, being musically demanding. I can't count the number of times I've told directors, "You have a great group. They'll do what you ask for, but you *DO* have to ask!"

105-107. Sharing And Changing Positions

Playing "your bells" you take care,
But I don't know if you're aware
Sometimes the best bet
Is to let go and let
Others ring that note, so you must share.

Some ringers stay put and stay still.
With "their bells" they remain fulfilled.
They won't understand
Sharing is a good plan.
Their assignments you'll find in their wills!

You'll help the program's situation
If you'll be brave and switch positions.
Attempt a new part.
No fear and take heart –
You'll be a better musician!

The unshakable rule is "If a bell can't be played musically and confidently as assigned, it must be reassigned." Each ringer's goal is to contribute to a musical whole that is meaningful and communicates well. The goal is *not* to play all bells in a given position. To be sure, we start by trying to play all the notes assigned, but if any note can't be played comfortably as assigned, it's time to share, reassign, or get a duplicate bell.

In a similar vein, I'm a firm believer in having ringers switch positions from piece to piece. Ringers have different comfort levels with this idea, and that should be respected. But trying a new position on even one title develops musicianship, technique, confidence, and team spirit.

108. Shut The World Out

We're busy, life brings more and more,
And on us more stresses are poured.
Put aside problems, fears;
Be HERE when you're here.
Let's ring! Check your bags at the door!

A recurring theme in this volume is my ever-growing dismay as I watch people get busier and busier and busier. The pace of their lives gets increasingly frantic, and the stress associated with that continually grows unhealthier and more debilitating. There are many blessings to an active, involved life, no question. The pervasive problem is keeping a sense of sanity and balance in making intelligent decisions about all that we take on in our lives.

Beyond the enormous impact this has on the scope of our handbell programs overall, the "superman or superwoman taking on more and more" syndrome has a seriously crippling effect on the ringer's ability to concentrate and be *present* in rehearsal. It's completely natural that the dizzying haze of an insanely busy life would make a person's mind cloudy and restless, uneasy, anxious, and unable to focus.

It's tremendously important to do what we can to make sure we are all HERE while we are here. This can be achieved through a time of meditation and prayer, an announcement and/or personal sharing time, and most importantly through simply being aware of the problem so that ringers can try to ready their minds for music-making even before they get to rehearsal.

Rehearsal time is severely limited. I've *never* heard a director or ringer say, "We always have plenty of time to rehearse our music." So find some way to help everyone in the group to be in the here and now. This might be by turning off the radio and taking some quiet time in the car on the way to practices and performances or maybe playing one or two less pieces this season to make room in rehearsal for time to reflect and focus – there are many ways to leave that frantic, whirling world outside. Check your problems and baggage and things that drag you down at the door. Come in and be *present* at rehearsal. Bring your enthusiasm and your willing, eager mind and spirit to bear on the music and the people that inspire you, and refocus on lifting up those who listen to what we've created.

109. Rehearsal Time Is For Rehearsing

At practice, there's so little time,
So use it to make music fine.
Do business, be social
Outside of rehearsal.
Between these things, best to draw lines.

As described in the previous lesson, there is great benefit to setting aside a few minutes of rehearsal time for focusing our minds and hearts on the music and on the present moment. As a further help with that, I believe that most socializing and all business matters should be engaged in outside of rehearsal. To be sure, there is a social aspect to every bell choir, and that is one of the reasons we love being in the program. For that reason, trying to eliminate social moments in rehearsal would be a useless and painful exercise. Still, rehearsal time is set aside for building and polishing our music, so it's important to make that the priority and to keep social matters in balance. As for business and logistical matters, I believe those should be taken care of outside of rehearsal as much as humanly possible. In an age of email and other convenient ways to share information, there's no reason to have business meetings at the cost of valuable practice time.

To be fair, some groups exist largely for social reasons and some groups are successful having short business meetings during rehearsals. That *only* works if the musical load is small enough to give time for these other elements. Again, I've never heard a director or ringer say, "We have too much time in rehearsal." Business discussions and social bonding are very important, no question, but make sure they don't interfere with the musical work that needs to happen during the all-too-precious rehearsal time.

110. Performing At Weddings

Bells at weddings are loved but they may
Get lost in the shuffle and fray.
Remember your role.
Keep sight of the goal –
Just five words – "It was a great day."

Handbell ringers and directors think of playing at a wedding service as "performing," and inherently, there's nothing wrong with that. I'm of the school of thought that there is no problem whatsoever with calling our presentations in worship services "performances." They *are* performances, in the sense of presenting polished, well-rehearsed music that communicates beauty and excitement. There is potential trouble with the word when the focus becomes earning applause and compliments over being a blessing and enhancement to the spiritual message and flow of the worship service. But I also believe there is nothing fundamentally wrong with the applause or other compliments, as long as the *primary goal* is to bring the hearts of worshippers into God's presence.

The wedding ceremony can have more elements of concert and performance than some general worship services, but it is, first and foremost, a worship service. So the music's primary role is to serve the spiritual celebration. There may be more bell music than in other services and certainly you want the quality of the music to be top-notch, as always. But remember that the main goal is to enhance a very special day in these people's lives. I've been surprised to hear ringers come away from playing at a wedding (or other worship services, for that matter) feeling disappointed that they didn't get more direct attention, had to play in the background for something else that was going on, and didn't feel appreciated enough generally. These attitudes, in my opinion, miss the point. What is THE highest compliment that you can hear after playing for a wedding? "It was a great day!"

111. Concert

In church, you play music galore.
It's fun, but you want to play more.
More music prepare,
Play a concert somewhere
And reach beyond the church door.

With the emphatic warning that you should always keep in mind the "do less and do it well" principle, preparing a concert can be very fulfilling and a lot of fun for both the bell choir and the audience. Clearly, if preparing extra music and/or spending time polishing music you've performed before causes stress and makes for problems in your ongoing program, this isn't the time to take on a concert. But if you've reached a point where you have some confident, solid material in your repertoire and can take on the demands of a recital with grace and enthusiasm, you have a wonderful opportunity to reach hearts with your music and spirit in a setting that extends beyond your regular worship program.

112. You're In Charge Of You

Especially when you're on tour,
You just want to do more and more.
Be sure to get rest
So that you'll play your best.
The "take care of yourself" job is yours.

Ringers can run themselves ragged by trying to do extra things while on a group trip or by socializing too much and not getting rest. Tours are, in a sense, a sleep-optional prospect. ☺ And one of the main purposes of a tour is to bring the members of a choir together socially and form group bonds. Still, remember that another primary purpose of a tour is to perform well, so some balance between activities and rest is essential to make sure the group is playing its best. After all, you traveled to show audiences what you can do!

113. Thank You

When considering all that they can do
As directors with hearts gifted and true,
It's really not hard,
Give a hug, send a card,
Just a little something to say thank you.

I've received numerous heartfelt compliments and expressions of thanks for my work as writer, clinician, and director. I'm sure this is true of most teachers and directors, so this limerick is not intended to paint a picture of leaders as poor unappreciated souls. Still, leaders put themselves out there week after week, dealing with the demands of the clock, the stresses involved in keeping track of the program's musical and logistical details, and overcoming the fears of being misunderstood (I am a particularly comfortable public speaker, but let me testify that the fear of offending someone or saying something utterly stupid or harmful constantly lurks in the background of even the most confident leader's work).

Directors have the same need as ringers to enjoy the music and the bell program and to be "fed" spiritually by companionship and a sense of belonging. A small word of thanks or acknowledgement for seeing to the details of the program or a compliment on adding a nice musical touch can mean the world to a director.

RESOURCES

114-116. Festivals/Workshops

It's worth the price of admission
To work with a handbell clinician
Who knows how to teach
And new heights to reach
And make you a better musician.

Don't let learning end, reach the "top."
The growth of your skills never stops.
Save up for the fees;
Find time, if you please,
And get yourself to a workshop!

Bells take over the biggest performance hall.
We get to do what we love best of all –
Ring bells for a day
And learn as we play!
Make sure you attend the next festival!

117. Copying Music

It's not just a little faux pas
When you writers' money withdraw.
More than talent they're giving –
They're making a living.
Making copies is breaking the law…

…EXCEPT when you purchase a license to do so! And with web publishing, that's what you are doing. The limited permission to make copies that you receive through purchasing the license is a *BIG* money-saver. This is the principle upon which Sonology Music and STEP are built (http://www.sonologymusic.com). One of the standard arguments against web publishing is that it encourages people to make illegal copies of music, but the opposite is the reality. Web publishing defines exactly when it is and is not legal to make copies and is therefore a great boon not only to ever-diminishing music budgets but also to the integrity of the industry as a whole.

118-119. Instant Music! Sonology/STEP

Life's crazy! You've fallen behind.
That last-minute piece you must find.
Instant music, that's right!
There are several websites –
Just order, download, and you're fine!

The price of music makes you queasy.
Sonology/STEP makes life easy!
It's the wave of the future.
Find music to suit your
Program online! It's a breeze! See?

Another HUGE advantage to availing yourself of web publishing is *instant handbell music!* Browse, select, order, download, print – you can be playing this music *the same day!* No more calling frantically to expedite an order, no more falling short in filling your bell choir's immediate programming needs. And the cost is *considerably* less than the music you order in the traditional fashion.

The best of these websites – widest selection, greatest ease of use, best customer support – is Sonology Music at http://www.sonologymusic.com. The Sonology catalog encompasses full choir music of every difficulty level and for all your handbell program needs. You'll also find the STEP (Solo To Ensemble Project) catalog which contains solos, duets, trios, quartets, and other ensembles for all experience levels and for the full range of worship and concert needs.

120-122. Not "Enough" Ringers – A Great Solution!

Of ringers you don't have "enough,"
So playing your music seems rough.
You'll be at your best;
Use music for less –
Play ensembles! Now, that's the stuff!

Your program's lost ringers this season.
Don't give up, 'cause you have no reason!
Choose music that's written
For fewer to fit in.
Ensembles and solos are pleasin'.

You've heard solos with no mis-step
And ensembles played with much pep,
So don't get disheveled.
Find songs at your level;
Start simple and go step by STEP.

STEP – the Solo To Ensemble Project – offers solos, duets,
trios, quartets, and other ensembles for all ability levels. Go to
http://www.sonologymusic.com.

123. Music In Motion

Bells are visual, so make the look
A priority as your group cooks
Up an artistic potion
Of "Music in Motion" –
The best journey you ever took!

Pikes Peak Ringers offers an instructional DVD entitled "Music in Motion" on the subject of visual presentation, available at http://www.pikespeakringers.com.

I highly recommend going through this course with me and PPR as your guide, taking your group on the musical adventure of exploring strong visual elements to make your music communicate better to your audiences and congregations. The "Music in Motion" DVD is filled with simple, accessible ideas about stances, techniques, movements, and visual style. It's a tremendous resource, the only one of its kind available on this crucial subject.

124. Recording

The process to make a recording
Can be, there's no question, quite boring.
The job falls to you
To make each take new.
Remember, you get a recording!

125. Recording And Licensing

When recording it's really not funny
To omit credit or paying money.
Licensing is the law
And the fee is quite small,
So record! The outlook is sunny!

Once a song has been recorded one time, publishers are *required* to issue mechanical licenses on all future recordings. The flipside is that your group is required by law to pay the proper mechanical licensing fees; this is *not* optional as it is part of how writers and publishers make their money. You are not asking for "permission" to record – you don't need permission. But you are asking for a mechanical license, and the fee you pay per title is affordable.

For more information, go to the Harry Fox Agency website, http://www.harryfox.com.

126. Trouble Getting A Mechanical License

Though it doesn't appear to make sense
Some publishers put up pretense,
Say "permission denied."
Then it's time to try
A "compulsory mechanical license."

Publishers sometimes make a show of denying a mechanical license for small projects, partly because they don't want competition with their popular recordings and partly because they don't want to mess with the detailed bookkeeping. They can say all they want that they are denying "permission" to make the recording, but you are not asking for permission and it isn't the copyright holder's role to give it. The law says that once a song has been recorded, publishers are *required* to issue a mechanical license.

If a publisher is giving you a hard time concerning a mechanical license, the law provides a recourse. It's called a "compulsory mechanical license" and essentially involves giving notice to the publisher that you are going to use the song on your recording and are sending them the statutory fee. Keep all documentation of your correspondence with the copyright holder, as well as a record of sending this final notice and the fee. With good record-keeping, you can consider your due diligence done.

For more information, go to the US Copyright Office website, http://www.copyright.gov.

PEOPLE

127. People

The bells in themselves may be elegant.
You ring amidst laughter and merriment.
The very best part
Of bells is the heart –
The PEOPLE are really the instrument!

128-129. Invest In Youth

Who will we pass the baton to
And writing and teaching pass on, too?
The future, in truth,
Is "invest in youth."
It's them our bell future belongs to.

Adults magic music can handle.
To some you just can't hold a candle.
But you know the truth –
Our future is youth,
So teach our young kids to ring handbells!

While the message of these two poems may seem obvious, in my opinion the bell world is offering nowhere near enough for children, youth, and college-age young adults. That is not meant as a criticism of the existing programs for these young people as there are some wonderful things happening. There just aren't enough of them. If you have the chance to expand your church bell program to include children and youth, to bring the bells into your local public schools and do some educating, to create festivals and workshops for youth ringers and their leaders – do it!

There are some doom-and-gloomers out there who are saying that the art of handbells is dying away. I wouldn't go that far, but there's no question that there are significantly less ringers now than there were some years ago. There are a number of reasons for this. Not surprisingly, I feel the reason that heads the list is that people are so busy! But another consideration that has an impact on our instrument is that nowhere near enough young people are creating music with bells in their hands.

Another reason on the list is that bell choirs are having a rough time finding their role in contemporary "praise and worship" services. I firmly believe that bell choirs involving ringers of all ages can easily find ways to participate in this style of worship. One of the cries of woe concerning contemporary worship is that so many young people are being drawn to it, and therefore are moving away from traditional music-making, including handbells. Does it strike anyone besides me that maybe the expression of these problems has provided its own answer? Get your youth ringing bells in these services!

130-133. Playing For People

I know you get scared, want to hide,
And listeners you just can't abide.
They love what you do,
And appreciate you.
Listeners ARE on your side!

Ringing for folks, don't be scared!
Remember that you are prepared!
Their appreciation,
Audience, congregation,
Means wonderful things you have dared!

Is it something important you're bringing
As your music to others is winging?
New places you take them
And happy you make them;
Let that be your focus when ringing.

The ministry of music's sound
Can lift hearts of those who are down.
You never know who
Has been touched by you.
Your impact can be quite profound.

One of the many teachers and collaborators for Pikes Peak Ringers is a professional opera singer named Judith Shay-Burns. In visiting our rehearsals and in working with us for concerts, she offered some remarkable insights concerning breathing while ringing, characterization of the music, and a great many other sophisticated elements of performance. But I think the most important thing, simple as it is, that she taught us is to remember that "We make people happy." People enjoy the heart, spirit, and personality of the music we create. When bogged down in the details and pressures of the bell program, it always pays to remember that we have something special to offer our listeners, that this crazy thing we do makes people happy!

134. What You Bring

What do you bring to the table?
Don't be in a hurry to label.
More experience or less,
What you bring is your best.
With a "yes" spirit, do what you're able.

135. No Man Is An Island

There's no place for egos in my band,
Prima donnas, or taking a high hand.
Though separate you seem,
You're part of a team.
In bells, "No man is an island."

("No man is an island." – John Donne)

136-137. Always Learn!

It's true that, in bells, volunteers
Are the backbone of ringing careers.
Train yourself, more you'll know
And through workshops you'll grow.
Always learn to improve through the years.

Never Arrive!

In music, you never "arrive."
You always continue to strive.
Where you are never rest,
Keep on stretching your best.
Keep commitment to your growth alive.

Always learn! Never arrive! I can't think of a more important mantra for handbell ringing. In fact, it's one of the vital tenets for life. A firm believer in not having an age prejudice, I've taught enthusiastic workshop and festival participants in their 80's and 90's, always with joyful results. One of the most rewarding handbell classes I ever taught was at an Elderhostel camp where my ringers were all complete beginners and almost all were over 70 years old, several over 80. Our final short concert may not have been highly polished, but it was joyful and communicated musically as effectively as any concert I've ever directed. That was entirely due to these wonderful people's willingness and eagerness to learn and learn and *learn some more!*

138. Smile!

The technical battles you've won,
So musically take it and run!
Your listeners should see
What a joy bells can be!
It's ok to smile and have fun!

It is permissible to smile when ringing handbells!

When someone asks you why you joined the bell choir, the answer is obviously "Because it's fun!" But then we get into the rehearsing and the technique and all the rest, and fierce concentration takes over and the smiles disappear.

People come to a service or concert to see you. I wish they came to hear you, but that's not really the case. Think about it: when you're getting ready to leave the house to go to your child's program at school, you say "Well, let's go see Johnny," you don't say "Let's go hear him."

The emotion you show through your body language and facial expression is the emotional message those watching will take with them after you play. If your face shows, say, abject terror, that's what gets communicated! ☺

Crazy as it sounds, it pays to actually practice facial expressions. This doesn't mean pasting a cheesy grin on your face – I think people can see right through that. But it does mean allowing your face to reflect the joy you find in ringing, even in rehearsal. Remember, what you rehearse is what you'll perform. So be sure people hear – and see! – the joy of ringing!

139. Focus

The right notes can be such a fight
When pressure is on, time is tight.
There's no hocus-pocus,
You just have to focus
And know your left hand from your right. ☺

140-142. Mentally Ready

When busy, our thoughts tend to rage
And wander. We don't need a "sage"
Saying "Bags at the door
You must check." Ready for
Rehearsal, your mind must engage.

Calm The Nerves

It's vital to put nerves at peace
And put congregations at ease.
Meditate, say a prayer,
Give a hug, or just share.
Confident music will please.

Prayer

We've all got distractions to spare
And spiritual focus is rare
When our lives are so busy
And we're in a tizzy,
So start your rehearsals with prayer.

Not every bell choir is a religious or spiritual organization. But if it's appropriate to the program, nothing centers people's minds and hearts for fine music-making better than prayer. If you are in an organization where prayer would not be appropriate, it's still a good idea to spend a few moments bringing everyone's focus to the music through a few words from the director, a simple short pause between "real life" and rehearsal, a hug break, a pep talk, etc.

In addition, I often ask ringers to "check their bags at the door," meaning they need to leave the concerns, stresses, and distractions of life outside the rehearsal room so we can focus our minds and hearts on the music.

SPIRIT

143. Music Nearest Heaven

If you've rung for one year or seven,
Eight, nine, or more than eleven,
You know as you ring
The music you bring
Is the music that's nearest to heaven.

("Bells – the music bordering nearest heaven." – Elia)

144. Music – The Language Of Spirit

Performance – how often we fear it!
But listeners, they love to hear it
When you create art
And ring from the heart.
Music is the language of Spirit.

I've heard "spirit" defined simply as "what connects me to you." Nothing can bring hearts closer together than the magic of music.

145. We've A Story To Tell

There's a tale to tell of God's great glory.
God has a strong message in store. He
Speaks love in that "space,"
From a heavenly place.
Think of ringing as telling His story.

Our ministry in bells is many-faceted, but one of the simplest aspects is that we create a "space," a place outside the "real world," that listeners occupy for the few minutes we play. This "space," this "time out of time" is a vital part of people's spiritual walk. When ringing, remember that you have the privilege of telling a story or offering a time of celebration or reflection or meditation to those who are listening. Maybe congregations and audiences will remember a great deal about the music, maybe they won't, but for the time that we play, we offer an opportunity to be "in the present moment," which brings listeners' hearts closer to God.

In fact, let's talk more about this...

146. The Place Where God Is Found

Music transcends the world's chatter,
Where minds are filled with noise and clatter,
Beyond time and space,
And into God's place,
Reminding souls what really matters.

I was sitting on my deck one afternoon, looking at the trees in our backyard and at the open park area behind our house. The wind was making some lovely tranquil patterns in the leaves as it sighed peacefully. I thought to myself, "God, I don't do this enough, take the time to just pause, reflect, and listen to you."

God does have a sense of humor. At that moment, a high school kid on a bicycle came zipping along the pathway through the park. He was clearly in a big hurry to get somewhere. And in one hand he had his cell phone; he was pedaling away furiously and texting someone at the same time!

How big a hurry are people in? How big a rush are we teaching our children to be in?

If one of the defining characteristics of God is that He exists out of time, our music ministry is more vital than it has ever been. Our job as musicians is to create a place out of time for the three or four minutes we play, a safe haven to set our minds and hearts apart from all of that frantic insanity that is the pace of the modern world.

I guess that youth's business with whomever he was texting just couldn't wait till he got home, or at least until he found a safe place to stop. That's what everyone's life has become – busy, frantic, stressed out, pulled in every direction, in many ways even physically, emotionally, and spiritually unsafe. Our music is not only enjoyable, fun, beautiful, exciting, and lovely. It is also *vital*, if only because it pulls people out of all of that, back to where God is, in the stillness and peace of our hearts.

147. Enthusiasm

We want enthusiasm seen,
All or nothing, with no in between.
"En" means "in" – that's not odd.
"Thus" is "Theos" – that's God.
"With God in us" – that's what it means!

That's right! That's really what the word "enthusiasm" means!
So when we say we're enthusiastic about handbells, and when
we play with enthusiasm, we are doing what we do with God
in us.

Cool, huh? ☺

148-149. Now, Here

Sometimes from our day we're just beat.
Remember that music's a treat.
Though your day was unpleasant,
Be here, in the present!
Your spirit makes your group complete.

Are you tired, life's going nowhere?
Is life filled with worry and care?
Respell "nowhere" to
"Now, here!" When you do,
These joyous moments you'll share.

Amazing things happen for you, the music, and the group when you put aside past concerns and future worries to share in the present moment.

150-153. Bells In Contemporary Worship

Worship has grown "modern," "blended."
To grow with it is recommended.
There's much you can do
In this worship that's "new."
Your bell program is FAR from ended!

"Contemporary" just means "now."
Bells have so much to offer, but how?
Look for music that's new,
That fits the venue
And those worshippers you can still WOW!

"New" worship is based upon song.
There are many ways to ring along.
Play a verse, chorus, chords,
Descants, process, and more.
In "new" worship, yes, we belong!

Learn some chords, which bells are in hand
As you read the chart. Yes, you can!
Don't be taken aback. This
Will just take some practice.
And then you can play with the band.

There are *plenty* of ways to use handbells in contemporary
and blended worship. Obviously, we can set up and play an
arrangement or original piece as we have for traditional
worship. But in modern worship, we have more opportunities
than ever to creatively enhance worship – playing with the
band, playing a verse or chorus of a song, ringing something
softly under prayer, ringing as a transition from one song to
another or one time in worship to another, processing, playing
a bell tree descant – the list has been far from exhausted.
Think outside the box, and soon you'll offer dozens of
effective ways to lift hearts to God in modern services.

154-155. Lift Every Note In Praise

When ringing, our handbells we raise,
Lifting spirits in magical ways.
It's more than just visual,
It's really quite literal –
We lift every note up in praise!

There's magic in ringing each chord
Together and in one accord.
There's nothing else near it,
The joy in the spirit
Of lifting each note to the Lord.

There is no other instrument that so vividly represents lifting
our hearts in praise to the Lord. What a wonderful ministry to
be a part of!

The Faithful Bell

There was an old bell in a tower
That faithfully rang out the hours –
Part of each celebration,
A sound of elation,
Reminder of God's strength and power.

Each time that its sound rose and swelled
It had a story to tell.
It sang in tones bright
Of God's peace, day and night.
I cherish that old faithful bell.

The sheer speed of life whirls around.
Life is frantic. Listen for the sound
Of that bell in its duty
Pealing forth in such beauty,
A still, small voice truly profound.

When life is too busy to tell
If God's really there, all is well!
I pause and I hear
The bell ringing God's cheer.
I cherish that old faithful bell.

From Me To You – A Final Word

People are busier now than ever before, busier than they were ten years ago, five years ago, last year. And all indications are that we will all be busier still in the future. A busy, active life is a blessing, IF it makes you happy. Everyone has a limit, though – we can't do everything. Each of us is just one person, and there is a point where we simply can't take on any more and be effective and joyful in what we are doing. Yet many of us continue to take on more...and more...and more...*and more*.

Handbells bring the message of a beautiful sound amid the cacophony of life, of peace amidst the frantic, uncontrolled nature of our schedules.

This is an important reminder to ringers because, as discussed previously in this volume, handbell choirs are volunteer organizations, which means that we fit our bell choir work into the cracks of our lives, in between family, work, trips, other commitments, and so on. I watch with a rapidly growing sense of dismay and discouragement as those crevices become smaller and smaller. Sad to say, many who participate in bell choirs aren't really an asset to the group as their hurried lives encroach on the time and energy necessary for the program. *Every* bell choir can benefit from periodically re-evaluating how much time is needed to be in the bell choir and how the ringers' schedules are affecting their work with the group.

The other important reminder contained in the magical sound of bells is for the listeners. God is found in the still, small voice. The mad pace of life continually pulls people further and further from God's presence, and that is tragic indeed when you consider how simple it is to reconnect with Spirit – just be still and know that He is God. How many people make time to do this, simple as it may be? The lovely tone of the bells sets listeners apart from the whirling, dizzying storm that is their lives, if only for a few moments. But how vital those moments are! They are the moments that bring us into the sunlight of the spirit.

If you are happy being busy, there's certainly nothing wrong with that. God encourages us to give what we can to the flow of life. I simply urge you to evaluate and pray about this often. Sometimes being active is a joy; but for the majority of people – at least the majority of the people that I've met – it's just stress and kills the peace of the soul. Do you *really* have the proper time and energy to devote to your handbell program? More importantly, are you finding moments of peace and silence in your life that bring you into the presence of God?

Being busy is fine, even very fulfilling, if it is in balance. The reality of the modern world is that being busy is *not remotely* in balance. It is an addiction vastly more common than addictions to alcohol, cigarettes, drugs, and so on. It is a damaging illusion, promising excitement and fun but delivering stress, lack of mental focus, bad health, strained work and relationships, restlessness, and discontent. It is a tragic condition of life that we are constantly encouraged to make worse by becoming busier and busier, more and more out of control, less and less content and peaceful. It is an appalling spiritual condition where we are never encouraged to find a more peaceful, happier, saner, more fulfilling way of life.

One of many simple ways to measure whether the busyness of your life is balanced is provided by the handbell choir. Are you contributing positively to the program, learning your music confidently and well, at peace that you are truly ready to present this music to your congregations and audiences? Are you missing rehearsal more than other ringers? Are you being honest with them and with yourself about absences and times that you arrive late or leave early? Is there restlessness and an undercurrent of stress in the bell choir caused by unresolved conflict or simply by not feeling well-prepared when you ring for people?

The handbell choir should be fun, exciting, with ringers eager to take on the next project and willing to put in the *time* necessary to create moments of beauty and joy. It is a tribe, a family that comes together because of the music and stays together because of love for the ministry and for each other. The handbell choir demands more concentrated *time* set apart for preparation and building of its repertoire than most other musical endeavors.

It's all lovely, freeing, happy – IF you really have the *time* to devote to it. And like so many elements of the handbell program, these are lessons that apply to many other avenues of life.

As you meditate on these matters, remember that God wants us, first and foremost, to be happy, joyous, and free.

Peace and blessings to you,
Kevin McChesney

Made in the USA
Middletown, DE
01 February 2019